W9-AYI-957

What do you Call a Rhyming Riddle!

A Hinky Pinky!

Written and illustrated by fifth-grade students
of St. Joseph Montessori School in Columbus, Ohio

Scholastic Inc.
New York Toronto London Auckland Sydney Mexico City New Delhi Hong Kong Buenos Aires

Kids Are Authors ®
Books written by children for children

The Kids Are Authors ® Competition was established in 1986 to encourage children to read and to become involved
in the creative process of writing. Since then, thousands of children have written and illustrated books as participants
in the Kids Are Authors ® Competition.
The winning books in the annual competition are published by Scholastic Inc. and are distributed by
Scholastic Book Fairs throughout the United States.

For more information:
Kids Are Authors®
1080 Greenwood Blvd., Lake Mary, FL 32746

Or visit our web site at:
www.scholastic.com/kidsareauthors

All rights reserved. No part of this publication may be reproduced, or stored in a retrieval system,
or transmitted in any form or by any means, electronic, mechanical, photocopying, recording,
or otherwise, without written permission of the publisher.
For information regarding permission, write to Scholastic Inc.,
Attention: Permission Department, 557 Broadway, New York, NY 10012.

Copyright © 2006 by Scholastic Inc.
Scholastic and associated logos are trademarks and/or registered trademarks of Scholastic Inc.

ISBN 978-0-439-91176-4
ISBN 0-439-91176-1

12 11 10 9 8 7 6 5 4 3

Cover and Book Design by Bill Henderson
Printed and bound in the U.S.A.

First Printing, June 2006

We dedicate this book
to the
St. Joseph
Montessori School
teachers
and our parents.

What's a Hinky Pinky?

Hinky Pinkies are fun word riddles that can be played almost anywhere at almost anytime. They have a clue that describes the two-word rhyming answer. For example:

What is a hink pink for a purple gorilla?

A grape ape!

But remember, the rhyming answer must have the same number of syllables in each word. One-syllable riddles are called Hink Pinks, two-syllable riddles are called Hinky Pinkies, and three-syllable riddles are Hinkety Pinketies. Now let's see if you can figure out these.

What is a hink pink for a cabinet from Holland?

Jared

What is a hinky pinky for an insane flower?

A crazy daisy!

What is a hinky pinky for falling buildings?

A tower shower!

What is a hinky pinky for an ill ship?

A sore-throat steamboat!

What is a hink pink for a dive with sharks?

Finlay

A grim swim!

13

What is a hinkety pinkety for a sorrowful Irish elf?

A woebegone leprechaun!

What is a hink pink for a cruel vegetable?

A mean bean!

Hot snot!

What is a hink pink for a foolish song?

A dumb hum!

What is a hinky pinky for a beautiful cat?

A pretty kitty!

How to Make a Hinky Pinky

1. The first step to making a hinky pinky is choosing your two rhyming words as your answer. For example: absurd blackbird. Remember, they need to rhyme and go together even if they're silly.

2. The next step is to find a good clue that describes your answer. For example: What is a crazy flying animal?

3. Next, you need to make sure that your answer matches the clue to your hinky pinky.

4. The last, but the best step, is to make a picture that fits your hinky pinky (without giving away your answer)!

NOW, TURN THE PAGE AND GET TO IT!

One-Syllable (Hink Pink)

tall	bend	blip	block
bawl	friend	zip	chalk
doll	lend	drip	clock
crawl	mend	trip	doc
small	spend	chip	dock
ball	trend	hip	flock
mall	blend	flip	talk
wall	end	quip	walk
shawl	send	snip	stock
stall		whip	smock
call		rip	crock
fall		lip	knock
hall		skip	Bach
		clip	rock
		slip	lock
		tip	jock
		dip	sock
			Jacques
			wok

Two-syllable (Hinky Pinky)

abuse	absurd	affect	begun
reduce	backward	collect	blowgun
caboose	blackbird	connect	grandson
deduce	concurred	correct	homerun
footloose	deferred	eject	outdone
masseuse	forward	expect	rerun
mongoose	jailbird	object	shotgun
produce	occurred	project	someone
vamoose	one-third	prospect	undone
papoose	preferred	respect	outrun
excuse	unheard	shipwrecked	redone
	transferred	subject	

Three-syllable (Hinkety Pinkety)

avenues
barbecues
interviews
revenues
kangaroos

brotherhood
fatherhood
Hollywood
likelihood
motherhood
neighborhood
sisterhood
understood

absolute
attribute
constitute
destitute
execute
institute
parachute
resolute
overshoot
substitute
troubleshoot

borderline
Frankenstein
intertwine
iodine
Palestine
porcupine
underline
undermine
storyline
valentine

Clue: _____

Answer: _____

Clue: _____

Answer:

Clue: _____

Answer:

Clue: _____

Answer:

Clue: _____

Answer:

MEET THE AUTHORS

Project Coordinator: Mr. William M. Reed
Top Row: Lewis Hagood, Keiko Wilkins, Anna Toborg
Row 2: Aaron Ault, Jared Ricardo, Brooke Lauer
Row 3: Evan Kozliner, Chris Perry, Jared Mohler, Finlay Hessler, Kendall Fugate-Laus, Kevin Smoot, Tommy Jones
Bottom Row: Ms. Sally Porter, Alex Toothman, Nikki Dean, Eleni Rigsby,
Adele Anderson, Kayla Barton, Mr. William M. Reed